low fat
kitchen

Women's Weekly
THE AUSTRALIAN

CONTENTS

AUSTRALIAN CUP AND
SPOON MEASUREMENTS
ARE METRIC. A
CONVERSION CHART
APPEARS ON PAGE 77.

These recipes prove those claims that diet food is boring food are completely wrong. Honestly, fresh, seasonal food is so full of flavour, and fruit drinks are so delicious, how can anyone think this type of food is boring? The whole family will love these recipes as well, so now you can feed everyone healthy food and hear no complaints.

Pamela Clark

Food Director

BREAKFAST FRY-UP

prep & cook time 15 minutes **serves** 4
nutritional count per serving 1.5g total fat
(0.1g saturated fat); 652kJ (156 cal);
22.5g carbohydrate; 8.9g protein; 7.6g fibre

4 small tomatoes (360g), quartered
2 tablespoons balsamic vinegar
300g mushrooms, sliced thickly
200g baby spinach leaves
⅓ cup coarsely chopped fresh basil
4 slices rye bread (180g), toasted

1 Preheat oven to 220°C/200°C fan-forced.
2 Combine tomato and half the vinegar in
small shallow baking dish. Roast, uncovered,
about 10 minutes.
3 Meanwhile, cook mushrooms, spinach
and remaining vinegar in large frying pan
until mushroom is tender and spinach wilts;
stir in basil.
4 Serve tomato and mushroom mixture
on toast.

BREAKFAST

scrambled eggs with asparagus

CRUMPETS WITH BERRY COMPOTE

prep & cook time **1 hour (+ refrigeration)** serves **4**
nutritional count per serving **1.7g total fat**
(0.1g saturated fat); 861kJ (206 cal);
40.1g carbohydrate; 5g protein; 4.8g fibre

1 cup (150g) self-raising flour
¼ teaspoon fine salt
¼ teaspoon caster sugar
¾ cup (180ml) warm water
¼ teaspoon dry yeast
cooking-oil spray
berry compote
125g strawberries, quartered
125g blueberries
150g raspberries
1 teaspoon finely grated orange rind
¼ cup (60ml) orange juice
2 tablespoons icing sugar

1 Make berry compote.
2 Meanwhile, sift flour, salt and sugar into medium bowl.
3 Combine the water and yeast in small heatproof jug. Add yeast mixture to flour mixture; stir until smooth.
4 Place four egg rings in heated oiled large frying pan; lightly spray each ring with oil. Fill each ring three-quarters full with mixture. Cook crumpets, over low heat, about 10 minutes or until surface is covered with burst air bubbles. Remove rings from crumpets, cover pan; cook crumpets about 3 minutes or until surface is firm. Remove from pan; cool on wire rack. Repeat with remaining mixture to make a total of eight crumpets.
5 To serve, toast crumpets; top with berry compote. Dust with extra sifted icing sugar, if you like.
berry compote Combine ingredients in medium bowl. Cover; refrigerate 1 hour.

SCRAMBLED EGGS WITH ASPARAGUS

prep & cook time **15 minutes** serves **4**
nutritional count per serving **2.8g total fat**
(0.8g saturated fat); 234kJ (56 cal);
1.4g carbohydrate; 6g protein; 0.8g fibre

340g asparagus, trimmed
cooking-oil spray
4 eggs
4 egg whites
⅓ cup (80ml) skim milk
1 medium tomato (150g), chopped finely
⅓ cup coarsely chopped fresh
   flat-leaf parsley

1 Boil, steam or microwave asparagus until tender; drain.
2 Meanwhile, lightly spray a large frying pan with oil. Whisk eggs, egg whites and milk in large jug. Cook egg mixture in pan, stirring, over low heat, until almost set.
3 Serve asparagus and scrambled eggs sprinkled with tomato and parsley.

crumpets with berry compote

strawberry hotcakes with blueberry sauce

STRAWBERRY HOTCAKES WITH BLUEBERRY SAUCE

prep & cook time **35 minutes** serves **4**
nutritional count per serving **2.6g total fat**
(0.7g saturated fat); 1814kJ (434 cal);
78.9g carbohydrate; 19.9g protein; 5.1g fibre

1 egg, separated
2 egg whites, extra
½ cup (125ml) apple sauce
1 teaspoon vanilla extract
2 cups (560g) low-fat yogurt
1¾ cups (270g) wholemeal self-raising flour
250g strawberries, hulled, chopped coarsely
blueberry sauce
150g blueberries, chopped coarsely
2 tablespoons white sugar
1 tablespoon water

1 Make blueberry sauce.
2 Using electric mixer, beat all egg whites in small bowl until soft peaks form. Combine egg yolk, apple sauce, extract, yogurt, flour and strawberry in large bowl; fold in egg whites.
3 Pour ¼ cup of the batter into heated greased large frying pan; using spatula, spread batter into a round shape. Cook hotcake, over low heat, about 2 minutes or until bubbles appear on the surface. Turn hotcake; cook until browned lightly on the other side. Remove from pan; cover to keep warm. Repeat with remaining batter.
4 Serve hotcakes with blueberry sauce.
blueberry sauce Place ingredients in small saucepan; bring to the boil, stirring constantly. Reduce heat; simmer, 2 minutes. Remove from heat; cool 10 minutes. Blend or process blueberry mixture until smooth.

cranberry and apple muesli

CRANBERRY AND APPLE MUESLI

prep time **5 minutes** (+ refrigeration) serves **4**
nutritional count per serving **3.2g total fat**
(0.6g saturated fat); 1133kJ (271 cal);
48.1g carbohydrate; 9.9g protein; 4.1g fibre

1½ cups (420g) skim-milk natural yogurt
1½ cups (135g) rolled oats
⅔ cup (160ml) unsweetened apple juice
½ cup (70g) dried cranberries
2 small green apples (260g), grated coarsely

1 Combine yogurt, oats and juice in small bowl; cover, refrigerate 3 hours or overnight.
2 Just before serving, stir cranberries and apple into muesli.

STRAWBERRY SOY SHAKE

prep time **10 minutes** serves **2**
nutritional count per serving **2.5g total fat
(0.4g saturated fat); 811kJ (194 cal);
26.7g carbohydrate; 14.6g protein; 3.5g fibre**

Blend 125g strawberries, 1½ cups reduced-fat
soy milk, 150g firm silken tofu and 1 tablespoon
honey until smooth.

TROPICAL WHEATGERM SMOOTHIE

prep time **10 minutes** serves **2**
nutritional count per serving **0.8g total fat
(0.2g saturated fat); 769kJ (184 cal);
25.3g carbohydrate; 11.1g protein; 10.1g fibre**

Blend ½ cup fresh orange juice, ½ peeled
and chopped small pineapple, 100ml strained
passionfruit juice, 250g low-fat yogurt and
1 tablespoon wheatgerm until smooth.
notes **You need about 5 passionfruit for this recipe.
Wheatgerm is available from health-food stores and
the health-food section of major supermarkets.**

FRUIT DRINKS

FRESH SUNRISE SMOOTHIE

prep time **10 minutes** serves **2**
nutritional count per serving **5.1g total fat**
(3g saturated fat); 1304kJ (312 cal);
53.8g carbohydrate; 10g protein; 6.4g fibre

Blend 1 coarsely chopped medium mango,
1 sliced medium banana, ½ cup fresh orange
juice, ½ peeled and chopped small pineapple,
and 1 cup rice milk until smooth.

BANANAS IN ALMOND MILK

prep time **10 minutes** serves **2**
nutritional count per serving **6.1g total fat**
(0.4g saturated fat); 1212kJ (290 cal);
48g carbohydrate; 10.5g protein; 4.9g fibre

Blend 2 tablespoons ground almonds,
2 tablespoons wheatgerm and 2 tablespoons
honey with 1 sliced medium banana and
1¾ cups reduced-fat soy milk until smooth.

corn fritters

BREKKY BEANS

prep & cook time **20 minutes** serves **4**
nutritional count per serving 2.8g total fat
(0.5g saturated fat); 1241kJ (297 cal);
43.3g carbohydrate; 17.3g protein; 13.4g fibre

1 medium brown onion (150g),
    chopped finely
2 cloves garlic, crushed
4 shortcut bacon rashers (60g),
    chopped finely
2 x 400g can diced tomatoes
2 tablespoons tomato paste
2 tablespoons wholegrain mustard
2 x 400g can white beans, rinsed, drained
⅓ cup coarsely chopped fresh
    flat-leaf parsley
4 slices rye bread (180g), toasted

1 Cook onion, garlic and bacon in heated
medium saucepan until onion softens. Add
undrained tomatoes, paste and mustard; cook,
stirring, until hot. Add beans; cook, stirring,
until hot. Stir in parsley.
2 Serve bean mixture with toast.

CORN FRITTERS

prep & cook time **20 minutes** serves **4**
nutritional count per serving 6.1g total fat
(1.4g saturated fat); 1476kJ (353 cal);
50.4g carbohydrate; 19.3g protein; 8.4g fibre

2 eggs
2 x 310g cans corn kernels, rinsed, drained
1 small red onion (100g), sliced thinly
1 cup (160g) wholemeal self-raising flour
⅔ cup (160ml) skim milk
cooking-oil spray
⅔ cup (130g) low-fat cottage cheese

1 Whisk eggs in medium bowl; stir in corn,
onion, flour and milk.
2 Lightly spray a large frying pan with oil. Pour
⅓ cup batter into heated pan; cook about
2 minutes or until bubbles appear. Turn fritters;
cook until browned lightly on the other side.
3 Serve warm fritters dolloped with cheese;
sprinkle with fresh dill or parsley, if you like.

brokky beans

BEEF AND VEGETABLE SOUP

prep & cook time 2 hours serves 4
nutritional count per serving 4.9g total fat
(1.5g saturated fat); 1074kJ (257 cal);
10g carbohydrate; 39.2g protein; 6.4g fibre

cooking-oil spray
500g lean diced beef
1 medium brown onion (150g),
    chopped coarsely
1 garlic clove, crushed
¼ cup (70g) tomato paste
1.5 litre (6 cups) water
2 bay leaves
2 medium carrots (240g), chopped coarsely
2 stalks celery (300g), trimmed,
    chopped coarsely
¼ small cauliflower (250g), cut into florets
1 large zucchini (150g), chopped coarsely
½ cup (60g) frozen peas
½ cup coarsely chopped fresh
    flat-leaf parsley

1 Lightly spray heated large saucepan with oil.
Cook beef, in batches, until browned. Remove
from pan.
2 Cook onion and garlic in same pan, stirring,
until onion softens. Add paste; cook, stirring,
2 minutes.
3 Return beef to pan with the water and bay
leaves; bring to the boil. Reduce heat; simmer,
covered, 1 hour. Uncover; simmer about
30 minutes or until beef is tender.
4 Add carrot, celery, cauliflower and zucchini;
simmer, uncovered, about 20 minutes or until
vegetables are tender. Add peas; stir until hot.
5 Serve soup sprinkled with parsley.

SOUPS
& SNACKS

chicken and corn soup

CHICKEN AND CORN SOUP

prep & cook time **40 minutes** serves **4**
nutritional count per serving **3.2g total fat**
(0.9g saturated fat); 769kJ (184 cal);
17.4g carbohydrate; 18.9g protein; 4.6g fibre

cooking-oil spray
2 trimmed corn cobs (500g), kernels removed
4cm piece fresh ginger (20g), grated
2 cloves garlic, crushed
4 green onions, sliced thinly
4 cups (1 litre) water
4 cups (1 litre) chicken stock
1 chicken breast fillet (200g)
1 teaspoon light soy sauce
1 egg white, beaten lightly

1 Lightly spray heated large saucepan with oil.
Cook corn, ginger, garlic and half the onion,
stirring, until fragrant. Add the water and stock;
bring to the boil.
2 Add chicken; reduce heat. Simmer, covered,
about 10 minutes or until chicken is cooked.
Cool chicken in broth 10 minutes. Remove
chicken; shred meat finely.
3 Return broth to the boil; add chicken and
sauce. Reduce heat; gradually stir in egg white.
4 Serve soup sprinkled with remaining onion.

butternut pumpkin soup

BUTTERNUT PUMPKIN SOUP

prep & cook time **35 minutes** serves **4**
nutritional count per serving **3.3g total fat**
(1.1g saturated fat); 715kJ (171 cal);
24.6g carbohydrate; 0.4g protein; 4.6g fibre

1 teaspoon olive oil
1 small leek (200g), sliced thinly
1 clove garlic, crushed
1 teaspoon ground cumin
½ teaspoon ground coriander
1kg butternut pumpkin, chopped coarsely
1 large potato (300g), chopped coarsely
3 cups (750ml) chicken stock
1 cup (250ml) water

1 Heat oil in large saucepan; cook leek and
garlic, stirring, until leek is tender. Add spices;
cook, stirring, until fragrant.
2 Add pumpkin, potato, stock and the water
to pan; bring to the boil. Reduce heat; simmer,
covered, about 20 minutes or until vegetables
are tender.
3 Stand soup 10 minutes then blend or process
soup, in batches, until smooth. Return mixture
to pan; stir until hot.

MEXICAN SHREDDED BEEF SOUP

prep & cook time **2 hours 40 minutes** serves **4**
nutritional count per serving **9g total fat**
(2g saturated fat); 1413kJ (338 cal);
25.9g carbohydrate; 34.3g protein; 7.4g fibre

500g piece beef skirt steak
2 litres (8 cups) water
1 bay leaf
6 black peppercorns
1 large carrot (180g), chopped coarsely
1 stalk celery (150g), trimmed,
** chopped coarsely**
1 tablespoon olive oil
1 medium brown onion (150g), sliced thickly
1 medium red capsicum (200g), sliced thickly
1 medium green capsicum (200g),
** sliced thickly**
2 cloves garlic, crushed
2 fresh long red chillies, chopped finely
1 teaspoon ground cumin
400g can crushed tomatoes
⅓ cup loosely packed fresh oregano leaves
1 trimmed corn cob (250g)
4 corn tortillas

1 Tie beef with kitchen string at 3cm intervals. Place in large saucepan with the water, bay leaf, peppercorns, carrot and celery; bring to the boil. Reduce heat; simmer, covered, 1½ hours. Uncover; simmer about 30 minutes or until beef is tender.
2 Cool beef in stock 10 minutes. Transfer beef to large bowl; using two forks, shred beef coarsely. Strain stock through muslin-lined sieve into another large heatproof bowl; discard solids, return stock to pan.
3 Heat oil in medium frying pan; cook onion, capsicums, garlic, chilli and cumin, stirring, until vegetables soften. Add onion mixture, beef, undrained tomatoes and ¼ cup of the oregano to pan with stock; bring to the boil. Reduce heat; simmer, uncovered, 10 minutes.
4 Cut corn kernels from cob. Add corn to soup; cook, uncovered, until just tender.
5 Meanwhile, preheat grill. Just before serving, cut each tortilla into eight wedges; place on oven tray, in single layer. Toast tortilla until crisp. Sprinkle remaining oregano over soup; serve with tortillas.

potato skins with tomato salsa

POTATO SKINS WITH TOMATO SALSA

prep & cook time 1 hour 25 minutes serves 4
nutritional count per serving 1.2g total fat
(0.1g saturated fat); 669kJ (160 cal);
30.4g carbohydrate; 4.3g protein; 4.4g fibre

8 small potatoes (960g), unpeeled
cooking-oil spray
1 teaspoon sea salt flakes
½ teaspoon ground white pepper
tomato salsa
6 medium egg tomatoes (450g), seeded,
    chopped coarsely
1 small red capsicum (150g), chopped coarsely
1 small red onion (100g), chopped coarsely
2 cloves garlic, sliced thinly
⅔ cup (160ml) bottled tomato pasta sauce
⅓ cup (80ml) vegetable stock
2 tablespoons red wine vinegar
1 tablespoon brown sugar
½ cup loosely packed fresh basil leaves, torn

1 Preheat oven to 200°C/180°C fan-forced.
2 Make tomato salsa.
3 Place potatoes in medium baking dish; roast,
uncovered, alongside tomato salsa, about
50 minutes or until tender. Cool.
4 Cut potatoes in half; scoop out flesh, leaving
skins intact (reserve potato flesh for another use).
5 Place potato skins, skin-side up, in single
layer on wire rack over baking dish. Lightly
spray with oil; sprinkle with salt and pepper.
Roast, uncovered, 20 minutes or until crisp.
6 Serve potato skins with tomato salsa.
tomato salsa Combine all ingredients, except
basil, in large baking dish; roast, uncovered,
50 minutes. Cool. Stir in basil.

GRILLED TOMATO GAZPACHO

prep & cook time 20 minutes (+ refrigeration)
serves 4 nutritional count per serving 1g total fat
(0.1g saturated fat); 414kJ (99 cal);
14.8g carbohydrate; 5g protein; 5.2g fibre

3 medium red capsicums (600g)
cooking-oil spray
6 medium egg tomatoes (450g), halved

grilled tomato gazpacho

1 medium red onion (170g), sliced thickly
4 cloves garlic, unpeeled
2 lebanese cucumbers (260g), seeded,
    chopped coarsely
2 tablespoons red wine vinegar
415ml can tomato juice
¼ cup (60ml) cold water
1 tablespoon finely chopped fresh
    flat-leaf parsley

1 Preheat grill.
2 Quarter capsicums, discard seeds and
membranes. Roast under hot grill, skin-side
up, until skin blisters and blackens. Cover
capsicum for 5 minutes then peel; chop
capsicum coarsely.
3 Meanwhile, lightly spray heated grill plate
with oil. Cook tomato, onion and garlic, turning
occasionally, until tender. When cool enough to
handle, peel garlic.
4 Stand soup 10 minutes then blend or process
capsicum, tomato, onion, garlic, cucumber,
vinegar and juice, in batches, until gazpacho is
smooth. Transfer to large bowl, cover; refrigerate
3 hours or until cold.
5 Stir the water into gazpacho. Serve gazpacho
sprinkled with parsley.

blueberry scones with vanilla frûche

ICY FRUIT KEBABS

prep time **15 minutes (+ freezing)** makes **8**
nutritional count per skewer **0.5g total fat**
(0g saturated fat); 464kJ (111 cal);
20.9g carbohydrate; 3.8g protein; 3.5g fibre

500g seedless watermelon, cut into
   3cm pieces
3 medium kiwifruit (255g), halved,
   sliced thickly
1 large mango (600g), cut into 3cm pieces
2 medium mandarins (400g), segmented
250g strawberries, halved
1 cup (280g) low-fat passionfruit yogurt
1 teaspoon finely grated orange rind
1 tablespoon orange juice

1 Thread fruit onto eight skewers; place onto
baking-paper-lined tray. Cover with foil; freeze
3 hours or overnight.
2 Combine yogurt, rind and juice in small bowl.
3 Serve kebabs with yogurt mixture.

BLUEBERRY SCONES
WITH VANILLA FRÛCHE

prep & cook time **30 minutes** makes **8**
nutritional count per scone **2.6g total fat**
(1.5g saturated fat); 832kJ (199 cal);
36.2g carbohydrate; 7.1g protein; 1.8g fibre

2 cups (300g) self-raising flour
2 tablespoons icing sugar
1¼ cups (310ml) buttermilk
150g blueberries
200g French Vanilla Frûche Lite

1 Preheat oven to 220°C/200°C fan-forced.
Grease shallow 20cm-round sandwich pan.
2 Sift flour and icing sugar into large bowl;
pour in enough buttermilk to mix to a sticky
dough. Fold in blueberries.
3 Gently knead dough on lightly floured surface
until smooth; use hand to flatten out dough to
a 3cm thickness. Cut eight 5.5cm rounds from
dough; place rounds, slightly touching, in pan.
Bake, uncovered, about 20 minutes or until
browned lightly; turn scones onto wire rack.
Serve with Frûche.

Icy fruit kebabs

BEETROOT

prep time **5 minutes** makes **2½ cups**
nutritional count per tablespoon **0.8g total fat
(0.3g saturated fat); 75kJ (18 cal);
1.9g carbohydrate; 0.5g protein; 0.6g fibre**

Blend or process 850g can drained beetroot
slices, one quartered garlic clove, ¼ cup sour
cream, 1 tablespoon tahini and 1 tablespoon
lemon juice until smooth.

TZATZIKI

prep time **5 minutes** makes **2 cups**
nutritional count per tablespoon **1.5g total fat
(1g saturated fat); 109kJ (26 cal);
2g carbohydrate; 1.2g protein; 0.1g fibre**

Combine 1 seeded coarsely grated lebanese
cucumber, 500g greek-style yogurt, 1 teaspoon
ground cumin and 2 tablespoons coarsely
chopped fresh mint in small bowl.

WATERCRESS AND YOGURT DIP

prep time **10 minutes** makes **1 cup**
nutritional count per ¼ cup **2.4g total fat**
(1.5g saturated fat); 222kJ (53 cal);
3.4g carbohydrate; 3.6g protein; 0.4g fibre

Blend or process 1 cup loosely packed
watercress sprigs, 1 teaspoon ground cumin,
¼ teaspoon cayenne pepper and ¼ cup yogurt
until smooth; transfer mixture to small bowl.
Stir in another ¾ cup yogurt.

WHITE BEAN AND GARLIC DIP

prep time **5 minutes** makes **1 cup**
nutritional count per ¼ cup **0.9g total fat**
(0.6g saturated fat); 138kJ (33 cal);
2.6g carbohydrate; 2.4g protein; 1.1g fibre

Rinse and drain 300g can white beans; blend
or process with ⅓ cup yogurt, 2 tablespoons
lemon juice and 1 quartered garlic clove until
smooth. Sprinkle with a pinch of ground cumin.

TOMATO, ZUCCHINI AND OREGANO SLICE

prep & cook time 1hour 10 minutes **serves** 4
nutritional count per serving 3.6g total fat
(1.2g saturated fat); 477kJ (114 cal);
3.1g carbohydrate; 16.0g protein; 2.3g fibre

250g cherry tomatoes
2 eggs
6 egg whites
⅔ cup (130g) low-fat cottage cheese
2 cloves garlic, crushed
1 large zucchini (150g), grated coarsely
⅓ cup coarsely chopped fresh oregano
60g baby spinach leaves

1 Preheat oven to 200°C/180°C fan-forced.
Grease deep 19cm-square cake pan; line base
and sides with baking paper, extending paper
5cm over sides.
2 Place tomatoes in pan. Roast 10 minutes.
3 Meanwhile, combine eggs, egg whites,
cheese and garlic in medium jug.
4 Remove tomatoes from oven; reduce oven
temperature to 160°C/140°C fan-forced.
5 Sprinkle tomatoes with zucchini and oregano;
pour over egg mixture. Bake about 45 minutes
or until set.
6 Cut slice into squares; wrap in plastic wrap
or baking paper. Pack spinach in an airtight
plastic container. Refrigerate slice and spinach
until ready to eat.

lemon grass and beef rice paper rolls

LEMON GRASS AND BEEF RICE PAPER ROLLS

prep & cook time 30 minutes serves 4
nutritional count per serving 3.8g total fat
(1g saturated fat); 690kJ (165 cal);
17g carbohydrate; 13.6g protein; 3.4g fibre

cooking-oil spray
180g beef fillet, minced finely
227g can water chestnuts, rinsed,
    drained, sliced thinly
10cm stick fresh lemon grass (20g),
    chopped finely
2 green onions, sliced thinly
1 fresh long red chilli, sliced thinly
1 tablespoon each lemon juice, kecap manis
    and fish sauce
12 x 21cm rice paper rounds
12 large fresh mint leaves
1½ cups (120g) bean sprouts
12 sprigs fresh coriander
lemon chilli dipping sauce
¼ cup (60ml) sweet chilli sauce
2 tablespoons lemon juice

1 Combine ingredients for lemon chilli dipping
sauce in small bowl.
2 Lightly spray heated frying pan with oil. Cook
beef, stirring, until browned. Stir in chestnuts,
lemon grass, onion, chilli, juice and sauces. Cool.
3 Dip one rice paper round into bowl of warm
water until soft; place on board covered with
tea-towel. Top with one mint leaf, one heaped
tablespoon of beef mixture, sprouts and a
coriander sprig. Fold and roll to enclose filling.
4 Repeat to make a total of 12 rolls.
5 Wrap rolls in plastic wrap; place dipping
sauce in airtight plastic container. Refrigerate
until ready to eat.

NOODLE AND MINT ROLLS

prep time 30 minutes makes 12
nutritional count per roll 1g total fat
(0.5g saturated fat); 163kJ (39 cal);
5.6g carbohydrate; 1g protein; 1.3g fibre

60g bean thread noodles
1 small carrot (70g), grated coarsely

noodle and mint rolls

200g wombok, shredded finely
1 tablespoon fish sauce
1 tablespoon brown sugar
¼ cup (60ml) lemon juice
12 x 17cm square rice paper sheets
12 fresh mint leaves

1 Place noodles in large heatproof bowl, cover
with boiling water; stand 10 minutes or until
just tender, drain. Using kitchen scissors, cut
noodles into random lengths.
2 Return noodles to same cleaned bowl with
carrot, wombok, sauce, sugar and juice; toss
gently to combine.
3 Dip one rice paper sheet into bowl of warm
water until soft; place on board covered with
tea-towel with a corner point facing towards
you. Place filling horizontally in centre of rice
paper, top with one mint leaf. Fold corner point
facing you up over filling; roll rice paper sheet
to enclose filling, folding in sides after first
complete turn of roll.
4 Repeat to make a total of 12 rolls.
5 Wrap rolls in plastic wrap; refrigerate until
ready to eat. Serve with a sweet chilli or soy
dipping sauce, if you like; place in an airtight
plastic container and refrigerate until required.

Prepare the filling the night before and keep, covered, in the refrigerator. Make the sandwiches or wraps the next morning.

CHEESE AND SALAD SANDWICH

prep time **10 minutes** serves **4**
nutritional count per serving **6g total fat**
(2.3g saturated fat); 911kJ (218 cal);
20.9g carbohydrate; 17.5g protein; 4.5g fibre

Combine 200g low-fat cottage cheese, ⅓ cup coarsely grated reduced-fat cheddar cheese, 1 cup shredded baby spinach leaves, 1 thinly sliced green onion, 1 finely grated small carrot, 1 tablespoon roasted sesame seeds and 2 teaspoons lemon juice in medium bowl. Sandwich 30g mesclun and cheese mixture between 8 slices of wholemeal bread; cut into halves or quarters. Wrap sandwiches in baking paper or plastic wrap; refrigerate until ready to eat.

DIJON CHICKEN AND SALAD WRAP

prep & cook time **25 minutes** serves **4**
nutritional count per serving **3.8g total fat**
(0.7g saturated fat); 932kJ (223 cal);
17.9g carbohydrate; 27.4g protein; 3.2g fibre

Lightly spray 2 chicken breast fillets with oil. Cook chicken in heated small frying pan; cool then shred coarsely. Combine chicken in medium bowl with 2 tablespoons skim-milk natural yogurt and 2 teaspoons dijon mustard. Divide chicken mixture between 4 rye mountain bread wraps; top with 40g baby spinach leaves, 2 thinly sliced small tomatoes and 2 coarsely grated small carrots. Roll up tightly to enclose filling; cut in half, if required. Wrap in baking paper or plastic wrap; refrigerate until required.

WRAPS & SANDWICHES

TURKEY AND CRANBERRY WRAP

prep time **5 minutes** serves **4**
nutritional count per serving **2.1g total fat
(0.4g saturated fat); 849kJ (203 cal);
27.6g carbohydrate; 16.7g protein; 2.5g fibre**

Spread 4 rye mountain bread wraps with ⅓ cup
cranberry sauce; top with 160g shaved turkey
breast, 60g snow pea sprouts and 60g baby
spinach leaves. Roll up tightly to enclose filling;
cut in half, if required. Wrap in baking paper or
plastic wrap; refrigerate until required.

TUNA, CELERY AND DILL SANDWICH

prep time **10 minutes** serves **4**
nutritional count per serving **6g total fat
(2.2g saturated fat); 1517kJ (363 cal);
42.5g carbohydrate; 29.9g protein; 8.4g fibre**

Drain and flake 2 x 185g cans tuna in springwater;
combine tuna with 4 finely chopped trimmed
celery stalks, ½ finely chopped small red onion,
⅓ cup low-fat ricotta cheese, 2 tablespoons
coarsely chopped fresh dill and 1 tablespoon
rinsed and drained capers in medium bowl.
Sandwich 40g baby spinach leaves and tuna
mixture between 8 slices of rye bread; cut into
halves. Wrap sandwiches in baking paper
or plastic wrap; refrigerate until ready to eat.

CAPSICUM, RICOTTA AND ROCKET PINWHEELS

prep & cook time **20 minutes** serves **4**
nutritional count per serving **3.5g total fat
(1.1g saturated fat); 640kJ (153 cal);
21.6g carbohydrate; 6.7g protein; 3.8g fibre**

**2 large red capsicum (700g)
1 tablespoon fresh lemon thyme leaves
2 teaspoons white wine vinegar
2 teaspoons lemon juice
1 teaspoon olive oil
½ teaspoon white sugar
2 slices wholemeal lavash bread (120g)
60g reduced-fat smooth ricotta cheese
40g baby rocket leaves**

1 Preheat grill to hot. Quarter capsicums; discard seeds and membranes. Roast capsicum under hot grill, skin-side-up, until skin blisters and blackens. Cover capsicum pieces with plastic or paper for 5 minutes; peel away skin then cut into thick strips.

2 Combine capsicum, thyme, vinegar, juice, oil and sugar in medium bowl.

3 Spread bread with cheese. Divide capsicum mixture and rocket leaves among bread; Roll up tightly to enclose filling; cut in half or quarters. Wrap in baking paper or plastic wrap; refrigerate until ready to eat.

note **Prepare the filling the night before; keep, covered, in the refrigerator. Make the wrap the next morning.**

Prepare salads the night before and keep, covered, in the refrigerator.

CHICKEN AND PEACH SALAD

prep time **10 minutes** serves **4**
nutritional count per serving **11.3g total fat
(2.4g saturated fat); 974kJ (233 cal);
8.5g carbohydrate; 22.9g protein; 4.4g fibre**

Combine 320g shredded cooked chicken,
6 cups shredded wombok, 1 cup shredded
fresh mint leaves and 4 small peaches, cut into
wedges, in large bowl. Combine ½ cup lime
juice and 1 tablespoon olive oil. Pack salad in
lunchbox; place dressing in separate airtight
plastic container; refrigerate. Just before eating,
drizzle salad with dressing.

POTATO, TUNA AND EGG SALAD

prep & cook time **15 minutes** serves **4**
nutritional count per serving **2.5g total fat
(2.4g saturated fat); 1150kJ (275 cal);
18.9g carbohydrate; 30.7g protein; 3.9g fibre**

Boil, steam or microwave 12 quartered baby
new potatoes and 200g trimmed and halved
green beans, separately, until tender; drain,
cool. Meanwhile, drain and flake 2 x 185g cans
tuna in springwater. Combine potato, beans
and tuna with ⅓ cup skim-milk natural yogurt,
6 thinly sliced green onions, 2 teaspoons finely
grated lemon rind, 1 tablespoon lemon juice and
2 tablespoons coarsely chopped fresh flat-leaf
parsley in large bowl. Pack salad in lunchbox;
refrigerate until required. Serve salad topped
with 4 quartered hard-boiled eggs.

LUNCHBOX SALADS

BEEF, MINT AND CUCUMBER SALAD

prep & cook time **25 minutes** serves **4**
nutritional count per serving **6.5g total fat
(1.7g saturated fat); 1375kJ (329 cal);
19.3g carbohydrate; 43.2g protein; 8.1g fibre**

Lightly spray 500g lean beef steak with oil.
Cook beef in heated small frying pan; remove
from heat. Cover; stand 5 minutes, then slice
thinly. Meanwhile, rinse and drain 2 x 300g
cans chickpeas. Combine beef and chickpeas
with 2 coarsely chopped lebanese cucumbers,
4 coarsely chopped medium tomatoes, 1 thinly
sliced small red onion, 1 cup coarsely chopped
fresh mint and ½ cup lemon juice in large bowl.
Pack salad in lunchbox; refrigerate until required.

TURKEY, FIG AND SPINACH SALAD

prep time **10 minutes** serves **4**
nutritional count per serving **3.8g total fat
(0.5g saturated fat); 502kJ (120 cal);
9.9g carbohydrate; 9.6g protein; 3.7g fibre**

Whisk 2 tablespoons raspberry vinegar and
2 teaspoons walnut oil in large bowl. Add
6 quartered large fresh figs, 100g baby spinach
leaves and 100g coarsely chopped shaved
turkey breast; toss gently to combine. Pack
salad in lunchbox; refrigerate until required.

VEGETARIAN PAELLA

prep & cook time 1 hour serves 4
nutritional count per serving 2.8g total fat
(0.6g saturated fat); 1680kJ (402 cal);
78.2g carbohydrate; 12.1g protein; 5.2g fibre

3 cups (750ml) vegetable stock
2 cups (500ml) water
pinch saffron threads
1 teaspoon olive oil
2 medium tomatoes (300g), seeded,
    chopped finely
1 medium red capsicum (200g),
    chopped finely
1 medium red onion (170g), chopped finely
2 cloves garlic, crushed
2 teaspoons smoked paprika
1¾ cups (350g) arborio rice
1 cup (120g) frozen peas
1 medium zucchini (120g), chopped finely
1 tablespoon finely chopped fresh
    flat-leaf parsley

1 Combine stock and the water in medium
saucepan; bring to the boil. Remove from heat;
stir in saffron.
2 Meanwhile, heat oil in large frying pan; cook
tomato, capsicum, onion, garlic and paprika,
stirring, until onion softens. Stir in rice then
stock mixture; bring to the boil. Reduce heat;
simmer, uncovered, without stirring, 20 minutes.
3 Sprinkle peas and zucchini evenly over surface
of rice; simmer, covered, about 10 minutes or
until rice is tender. Remove from heat; stand,
covered, 5 minutes before serving. Serve paella
sprinkled with parsley.

MAINS

moussaka stack with lemon-yogurt dressing

MOUSSAKA STACK WITH LEMON-YOGURT DRESSING

prep & cook time 30 minutes serves 4
nutritional count per serving 7g total fat
(2.3g saturated fat); 978kJ (234 cal);
13g carbohydrate; 25.8g protein; 6.3g fibre

1 medium brown onion (150g),
   chopped finely
2 cloves garlic, crushed
2 tablespoons beef stock
350g lean beef mince
2 medium tomatoes (300g),
   chopped coarsely
½ teaspoon ground cinnamon
½ teaspoon ground nutmeg
1 cup (250ml) beef stock, extra
⅓ cup coarsely chopped fresh
   flat-leaf parsley
⅓ cup coarsely chopped fresh basil
2 medium eggplants (600g)
2 small red capsicums (300g), quartered
½ cup (140g) skim-milk natural yogurt
1 tablespoon finely grated lemon rind
2 tablespoons lemon juice
40g baby rocket leaves

1 Cook onion, garlic and the stock in medium
frying pan until onion softens. Add mince,
tomato and spices; cook, stirring, until beef is
browned. Add extra stock; bring to the boil.
Reduce heat; simmer, uncovered, about
5 minutes or until liquid is absorbed. Remove
from heat; stir in herbs.
2 Meanwhile, slice each eggplant lengthways
into 6 slices; discard two outside pieces. Cook
eggplant and capsicum on heated grill plate (or
grill or barbecue) until browned and tender.
3 Combine yogurt, rind and juice in small jug.
4 Stack beef mixture, eggplant, capsicum and
rocket on serving plates; drizzle with dressing.

BARBECUED CHILLI PRAWN AND NOODLE SALAD

prep & cook time 35 minutes serves 4
nutritional count per serving 5.9g total fat
(2.6g saturated fat); 1145kJ (274 cal);
21.4g carbohydrate; 30.6g protein; 5g fibre

barbecued chilli prawn and noodle salad

100g bean thread noodles
1kg uncooked medium king prawns
1 teaspoon finely grated lime rind
1 clove garlic, crushed
2cm piece fresh ginger (10g), grated
2 tablespoons sweet chilli sauce
2 tablespoons lime juice
1 tablespoon fish sauce
1 small red capsicum (150g), sliced thinly
1 medium carrot (120g), cut into matchsticks
1 small red onion (100g), sliced thinly
150g snow peas, trimmed, sliced thinly
1 cup firmly packed fresh coriander leaves

1 Place noodles in heatproof bowl, cover with
boiling water; stand until tender, drain.
2 Meanwhile, shell and devein prawns, leaving
tails intact. Combine prawns, rind, garlic, ginger
and half the sweet chilli sauce in medium bowl.
Cook prawns on heated oiled grill plate (or grill
or barbecue) until changed in colour.
3 Combine prawns, noodles, remaining sweet
chilli sauce and remaining ingredients in large
bowl; toss gently.

MEDITERRANEAN WHITE FISH WITH BEANS AND OLIVES

prep & cook time **25 minutes** serves **4**
nutritional count per serving **5.5g total fat**
(1.6g saturated fat); 1279kJ (306 cal);
14.9g carbohydrate; 45.9g protein; 5.7g fibre

cooking-oil spray
800g firm white fish fillets, skin on
250g cherry tomatoes, halved
420g can four-bean mix, rinsed, drained
¼ cup (60ml) lemon juice
¼ cup (60ml) vegetable stock
½ cup (60g) seeded black olives,
chopped coarsely
½ cup coarsely chopped fresh
flat-leaf parsley

1 Lightly spray heated large frying pan with oil.
Cook fish, skin-side down, about 7 minutes or
until skin is crisp and fish is cooked as you like.
Remove fish from pan; cover.
2 Cook tomato in same pan until softened. Add
beans, juice and stock to pan; bring to the boil.
Add olives; cook, stirring, until hot. Stir in parsley.
3 Serve fish with bean mixture.

note **We used blue-eye fillets in this recipe.**

chilli con carne

CHILLI CON CARNE

prep & cook time 40 minutes serves 4
nutritional count per serving 8.1g total fat
(2.6g saturated fat); 1643kJ (393 cal);
45.1g carbohydrate; 29.8g protein; 8.6g fibre

⅔ cup (130g) brown rice
cooking-oil spray
1 medium brown onion (150g),
    chopped finely
2 cloves garlic, crushed
360g lean beef mince
2 teaspoons ground cumin
2 teaspoons dried chilli flakes
2 x 400g cans diced tomatoes
⅓ cup (95g) tomato paste
1 cup (250ml) beef stock
300g can four bean mix, rinsed, drained
⅓ cup (95g) skim-milk natural yogurt
½ cup coarsely chopped fresh
    flat-leaf parsley

1 Cook rice in medium saucepan of boiling
water until tender; drain.
2 Meanwhile, spray medium frying pan with
cooking oil; cook onion and garlic over heat,
stirring, until onion softens. Add beef and
spices; cook, stirring, until beef is browned.
3 Add undrained tomatoes, paste and stock;
bring to the boil. Reduce heat; simmer, covered,
10 minutes. Uncover; simmer about 10 minutes
or until mixture thickens slightly. Stir in beans.
4 Serve rice and chilli con carne topped with
yogurt; sprinkle with parsley.

linguine marinara

LINGUINE MARINARA

prep & cook time 25 minutes serves 4
nutritional count per serving 7.4g total fat
(2g saturated fat); 2253kJ (539 cal);
61g carbohydrate; 52.9g protein; 6.5g fibre

300g linguine pasta
800g marinara mix
1 medium brown onion (150g), chopped finely
3 cloves garlic, crushed
2 fresh small red thai chillies, chopped finely
2 x 400g cans diced tomatoes
⅔ cup coarsely chopped fresh
    flat-leaf parsley

1 Cook pasta in large saucepan of boiling
water until tender; drain.
2 Meanwhile, cook marinara mix in heated
large frying pan, stirring, 2 minutes; drain.
3 Add onion, garlic and chilli to same heated
pan; cook, stirring, about 5 minutes or until
onion softens. Add undrained tomatoes; cook,
5 minutes. Return seafood to pan; cook, stirring
occasionally, about 2 minutes. Stir in parsley.
4 Serve pasta with marinara sauce.

SPICED LAMB CUTLETS WITH TOMATO AND PARSLEY SALAD

prep & cook time **25 minutes** serves **4**
nutritional count per serving **9.6g total fat**
(3.2g saturated fat); 807kJ (193 cal);
2.5g carbohydrate; 22.7g protein; 2g fibre

2 teaspoons ground cumin
2 teaspoons ground coriander
12 french-trimmed lamb cutlets (600g)
4 medium egg tomatoes (300g), quartered
1 lebanese cucumber (130g),
    chopped coarsely
½ cup (100g) reduced-fat cottage cheese
1 cup loosely packed fresh
    flat-leaf parsley leaves
2 teaspoons olive oil
2 tablespoons red wine vinegar
1 clove garlic, crushed

1 Combine spices and lamb in medium bowl.
2 Cook lamb and tomato, in batches, on heated oiled grill plate (or grill or barbecue).
3 Combine tomato with remaining ingredients in medium bowl to make salad.
4 Serve lamb with tomato and parsley salad.

beetroot risotto with rocket

BEETROOT RISOTTO
WITH ROCKET

prep & cook time **1 hour 15 minutes** serves **4**
nutritional count per serving **7.6g total fat**
(2.1g saturated fat); 1643kJ (393 cal);
69.4g carbohydrate; 11.5g protein; 4.1g fibre

2 medium beetroot (350g), peeled,
  grated coarsely
3 cups (750ml) vegetable stock
3 cups (750ml) water
1 tablespoon olive oil
1 large brown onion (200g), chopped finely
2 cloves garlic, crushed
1½ cups (300g) arborio rice
¼ cup (20g) grated parmesan cheese
50g baby rocket leaves
1 tablespoon finely chopped fresh
  flat-leaf parsley

1 Combine beetroot, stock and the water in
large saucepan; bring to the boil. Reduce heat;
simmer, uncovered.
2 Meanwhile, heat oil in large saucepan; cook
onion and garlic, stirring, until onion softens.
Add rice; stir rice to coat in onion mixture. Stir
in 1 cup simmering beetroot mixture; cook,
stirring, over low heat until liquid is absorbed.
Continue adding beetroot mixture in 1-cup
batches, stirring, until liquid is absorbed after
each addition. Total cooking time should be
about 35 minutes or until rice is just tender;
gently stir in cheese.
3 Serve beetroot risotto topped with combined
rocket and parsley.

herb and tomato fish bundles

HERB AND TOMATO
FISH BUNDLES

prep & cook time **30 minutes** serves **4**
nutritional count per serving **3.4g total fat**
(0.9g saturated fat); 493kJ (118 cal);
1g carbohydrate; 20.6g protein; 0.6g fibre

4 x 100g firm white fish fillets
125g cherry tomatoes, halved
1 tablespoon rinsed, drained baby capers
4 fresh thyme sprigs
2 tablespoons white balsamic vinegar
1 teaspoon olive oil

1 Preheat oven to 200°C/180°C fan-forced.
2 Place each fillet on 20cm squares of baking
paper or foil. Divide tomato, capers, thyme,
vinegar and oil over fish pieces. Gather corners
of baking paper together above fish; twist to
enclose securely.
3 Place parcels on oven tray; bake 15 minutes.
Stand fish 5 minutes before serving.
serve with rocket salad.
note We used barramundi fillets in this recipe, but
you can use any firm fish fillets you like.

HERBED RICOTTA RAVIOLI WITH TOMATO SALSA

prep & cook time **35 minutes** serves **4**
nutritional count per serving **3.4g total fat**
(1.3g saturated fat); 447kJ (107 cal);
4.6g carbohydrate; 12.2g protein; 4.8g fibre

500g spinach, trimmed
⅓ cup (80g) reduced-fat ricotta cheese
1 egg white
1 tablespoon finely chopped fresh basil
2 teaspoons finely chopped fresh mint
1 teaspoon finely chopped fresh rosemary
24 wonton wrappers
tomato salsa
4 large egg tomatoes (360g), chopped finely
¼ cup loosely packed fresh baby basil leaves
1 tablespoon white balsamic vinegar
½ teaspoon olive oil

1 Boil, steam or microwave spinach until wilted; rinse under cold water, drain. When cool enough to handle, squeeze excess liquid from spinach; shred spinach finely.

2 Combine cheese, egg white, herbs and spinach in medium bowl. Divide spinach mixture among half the wonton wrappers; brush around edges with a little water. Top with remaining wrappers; press around edges firmly to seal.

3 Place four ravioli in large baking-paper-lined bamboo steamer; cook over large saucepan of simmering water about 5 minutes or until cooked through. Cover to keep warm. Repeat with remaining ravioli.

4 Meanwhile, make tomato salsa. Serve ravioli topped with tomato salsa.

tomato salsa Combine ingredients in small bowl.

spinach, tomato and prosciutto wholegrain pizza

SPINACH, TOMATO AND PROSCIUTTO WHOLEGRAIN PIZZA

prep & cook time 40 minutes (+ standing) serves 6
nutritional count per serving 6.5g total fat
(3g saturated fat); 1547kJ (370 cal);
55.7g carbohydrate; 18g protein; 7.4g fibre

⅓ cup (55g) finely cracked buckwheat
¼ cup (40g) burghul
1 cup (250ml) warm water
1 teaspoon caster sugar
8g sachet dried yeast
1½ cups (225g) plain flour
1 cup (160g) wholemeal plain flour
⅔ cup (170g) bottled tomato pasta sauce
1 cup (100g) grated mozzarella cheese
80g baby spinach leaves, trimmed
250g grape tomatoes, halved
8 slices prosciutto (120g), chopped coarsely

1 Combine buckwheat and burghul in medium heatproof bowl; cover with boiling water. Cover; stand 30 minutes. Rinse under cold water; drain.
2 Combine the warm water, sugar and yeast in small jug. Stand in warm place about 10 minutes or until frothy.
3 Combine buckwheat mixture in large bowl with flours. Add yeast mixture; mix to a soft dough. Knead dough on floured surface about 10 minutes or until smooth and elastic; place in lightly greased large bowl, cover. Stand in warm place about 1 hour or until doubled in size.
4 Preheat oven to 220°C/200°C fan-forced; grease two pizza trays or oven trays.
5 Divide dough in half. Roll halves on floured surface into 30cm rounds; place on trays.
6 Spread pizza bases with sauce, sprinkle with half the cheese; top with spinach, tomato and prosciutto then sprinkle with remaining cheese. Bake, uncovered, about 20 minutes or until top is browned lightly and bases are crisp.

OCEAN TROUT WITH THREE-BEAN SALAD AND BUTTERMILK DRESSING

prep & cook time 35 minutes serves 4
nutritional count per serving 8.3g total fat
(1.9g saturated fat); 1267kJ (303 cal);
20.1g carbohydrate; 30.7g protein; 11.1g fibre

ocean trout, with three-bean salad
and buttermilk dressing

400g ocean trout fillets
2 teaspoons finely grated lime rind
2 cloves garlic, crushed
400g baby new potatoes, quartered
200g green beans, trimmed, halved
200g yellow beans, trimmed, halved
300g frozen broad beans, thawed, peeled
1 cup (120g) frozen peas
buttermilk dressing
⅓ cup (80ml) buttermilk
2 tablespoons lime juice
1 tablespoon finely chopped fresh mint

1 Make buttermilk dressing.
2 Preheat oven to 200°C/180°C fan-forced. Line oiled oven tray with baking paper.
3 Rub fish with combined rind and garlic; place on tray. Roast about 15 minutes. Cool; flake fish.
4 Boil, steam or microwave potatoes until tender. Place green and yellow beans in saucepan of boiling water; simmer until tender. Add broad beans and peas for last 2 minutes of cooking time; drain, cool 5 minutes.
5 Combine fish with vegetables and dressing in large bowl.
buttermilk dressing Combine ingredients in screw-top jar; shake well.

BALSAMIC-SEARED STEAK WITH KIPFLERS AND MUSHROOMS

prep & cook time 30 minutes (+ refrigeration)
serves 4 nutritional count per serving 13.7g total fat
(4.3g saturated fat); 2165kJ (518 cal);
40.8g carbohydrate; 54.2g protein; 8.4g fibre

¼ cup (60ml) balsamic vinegar
2 cloves garlic, crushed
4 beef scotch fillet steaks (800g)
1kg kipfler potatoes, quartered lengthways
1 tablespoon olive oil
500g flat mushrooms, sliced thickly
2 tablespoons dry red wine
1 tablespoon plum jam
1 tablespoon cornflour
¾ cup (180ml) beef stock

1 Combine vinegar and garlic in medium bowl, add beef; toss beef to coat in marinade. Cover; refrigerate 3 hours or overnight.
2 Preheat oven to 200°C/180°C fan-forced.
3 Place potato, in single layer, in large shallow baking dish; drizzle with oil. Roast, uncovered, stirring occasionally, about 30 minutes or until browned lightly and crisp.
4 Meanwhile, cook steaks on heated oiled grill plate (or grill or barbecue) until cooked as desired. Cover to keep warm.
5 Cook mushrooms on same heated grill plate until just tender.
6 Place wine in small saucepan; bring to the boil. Add jam and blended cornflour and stock; stir until sauce boils and thickens slightly. Serve steaks with mushrooms, potato and sauce.

pumpkin and split pea tagine

PUMPKIN AND SPLIT PEA TAGINE

prep & cook time **1 hour** serves **4**
nutritional count per serving **7g total fat**
(1.5g saturated fat); 1484kJ (355 cal);
54.5g carbohydrate; 19.1g protein; 11g fibre

1 cup (200g) green split peas
1 tablespoon olive oil
1 medium brown onion (150g), chopped finely
2 cloves garlic, crushed
2 teaspoons ground coriander
2 teaspoons ground cumin
2 teaspoons ground ginger
1 teaspoon sweet paprika
1 teaspoon ground allspice
1kg pumpkin, diced into 3cm pieces
425g can crushed tomatoes
1 cup (250ml) water
1 cup (250ml) vegetable stock
2 tablespoons honey
200g green beans, trimmed, chopped coarsely
¼ cup coarsely chopped fresh coriander

1 Cook split peas in medium saucepan of
boiling water, uncovered, until just tender;
drain. Rinse under cold water; drain.
2 Heat oil in large saucepan; cook onion, stirring,
until softened. Add garlic and spices; cook,
stirring, about 2 minutes or until fragrant. Add
pumpkin; stir to coat in spice mixture.
3 Stir in undrained tomatoes, the water and
stock; bring to the boil. Simmer, uncovered, about
20 minutes or until pumpkin is just tender. Stir
in honey then beans and split peas; simmer,
uncovered, about 10 minutes or until beans are
just tender. Remove from heat; stir in coriander.
serve with **steamed couscous**.

HONEY DIJON CHICKEN WITH CREAMY CELERY AND FENNEL SLAW

prep & cook time **50 minutes** serves **4**
nutritional count per serving **8.8g total fat**
(2.9g saturated fat); 1371kJ (328 cal);
21.2g carbohydrate; 40.8g protein; 4.9g fibre

2 tablespoons honey
2 teaspoons dijon mustard
4 small chicken breast fillets (680g)

honey dijon chicken with
creamy celery and fennel slaw

creamy fennel and celery slaw
2 medium fennel bulbs (600g)
3 stalks celery (450g), trimmed, sliced thinly
¼ cup chopped chopped fresh
   flat-leaf parsley
2 teaspoons dijon mustard
2 tablespoons lemon juice
2 tablespoons light sour cream
2 cloves garlic, crushed
¼ cup (75g) low-fat mayonnaise

1 Combine honey and mustard in small bowl.
Brush chicken, both sides, with half the honey
mixture; cook chicken, in batches, in heated
oiled large frying pan about 15 minutes or
until cooked through, brushing with remaining
honey mixture.
2 Make creamy fennel and celery slaw.
3 Serve chicken with slaw; sprinkle with
reserved fennel tips.
creamy fennel and celery slaw Trim fennel,
reserving about 1 tablespoon of the tips
(discard the rest). Slice fennel thinly; combine
with celery and parsley in large bowl. Combine
remaining ingredients in small bowl, pour over
slaw mixture; toss gently.

ginger teriyaki beef

BARLEY RISOTTO WITH CHICKEN AND TARRAGON

prep & cook time **1 hour** serves **4**
nutritional count per serving **9.7g total fat**
(1.9g saturated fat); 1584kJ (379 cal);
31.6g carbohydrate; 38g protein; 9.8g fibre

1 tablespoon olive oil
500g chicken breast fillets, sliced thinly
3 cups (750ml) chicken stock
2 cups (500ml) water
1 medium brown onion (150g), chopped finely
1 clove garlic, crushed
2 medium leeks (700g), sliced thinly
¾ cup (150g) pearl barley
⅓ cup (80ml) dry white wine
1 cup (120g) frozen peas
2 tablespoons finely shredded fresh tarragon

1 Heat half the oil in large saucepan; cook chicken, in batches, until browned lightly and cooked through. Remove from pan; cover to keep warm.
2 Meanwhile, combine stock and the water in large saucepan; bring to the boil. Reduce heat; simmer, covered.
3 Heat remaining oil in cleaned pan; cook onion, garlic and leek, stirring, until onion softens. Add barley; stir to combine with onion mixture. Add wine; cook, stirring, until almost evaporated. Stir in ½ cup simmering stock mixture; cook, stirring, over low heat until liquid is absorbed. Continue adding stock mixture, in ½-cup batches, stirring until absorbed after each addition. Total cooking time should be about 30 minutes or until barley is just tender.
4 Add chicken and peas to risotto; cook, stirring, until peas are just tender. Remove from heat; stir in tarragon.

GINGER TERIYAKI BEEF

prep & cook time **20 minutes** serves **4**
nutritional count per serving **3.9g total fat**
(1.1g saturated fat); 727kJ (174 cal);
15.7g carbohydrate; 15.5g protein; 5.3g fibre

2 tablespoons teriyaki sauce
2 tablespoons hoisin sauce
1 tablespoon mirin
½ teaspoon peanut oil
200g beef fillet, sliced thinly
1 large red capsicum (350g), sliced thinly
200g snow peas, trimmed, sliced thinly
  lengthways
1 medium carrot (120g), cut into matchsticks
115g baby corn, quartered lengthways
4cm piece fresh ginger (20g), sliced thinly
2 tablespoons water

1 Combine sauces and mirin in small jug.
2 Heat oil in wok; stir-fry beef until browned. Remove from wok.
3 Add capsicum, peas, carrot, corn, ginger and the water to wok; stir-fry until carrot is almost tender. Return beef to wok with sauce mixture; stir-fry until hot.
serve with **steamed jasmine rice**.

barley risotto with chicken and tarragon

veal cutlets with onion marmalade

VEAL CUTLETS WITH ONION MARMALADE

prep & cook time 1 hour (+ refrigeration) serves 4
nutritional count per serving 11.7g total fat
(4.1g saturated fat); 1965kJ (470 cal);
50.8g carbohydrate; 40.1g protein; 10.4g fibre

2 teaspoons olive oil
1 clove garlic, crushed
1 teaspoon cracked black pepper
4 veal cutlets (680g)
20g butter
2 large red onions (600g), sliced thinly
⅓ cup (75g) firmly packed brown sugar
¼ cup (60ml) cider vinegar
2 tablespoons orange juice
2 teaspoons finely chopped fresh rosemary
2 cobs corn (800g), trimmed, cut into
    3cm pieces
500g asparagus, trimmed

1 Combine oil, garlic and pepper in large bowl,
add veal; toss veal to coat in marinade. Cover;
refrigerate until required.
2 Meanwhile, heat butter in medium frying pan;
cook onion, stirring, until soft and browned
lightly. Add sugar, vinegar and juice; cook, stirring,
about 15 minutes or until onion caramelises.
Remove from heat; stir in rosemary.
3 Cook corn and asparagus, in batches, on
heated oiled grill plate until browned lightly and
cooked as desired; cover to keep warm.
4 Cook veal on same grill plate until cooked
as desired. Serve veal, corn and asparagus
topped with onion marmalade.

HERB-STUFFED CHICKEN WITH TOMATO SALAD

prep & cook time 50 minutes serves 4
nutritional count per serving 7.4g total fat
(1.7g saturated fat); 1066kJ (255 cal);
3.4g carbohydrate; 42.9g protein; 3.6g fibre

¼ cup finely chopped fresh basil
1 tablespoon finely chopped fresh oregano
2 teaspoons fresh lemon thyme
2 cloves garlic, crushed
1 tablespoon finely grated lemon rind

herb-stuffed chicken with tomato salad

4 small chicken breast fillets (680g)
4 slices prosciutto (60g)
250g cherry tomatoes
250g teardrop tomatoes
150g baby spinach leaves
½ cup coarsely chopped fresh basil
2 tablespoons red wine vinegar
2 teaspoons olive oil

1 Preheat oven to 180°C/160°C fan-forced.
2 Combine finely chopped basil, oregano,
thyme, garlic and rind in small bowl. Using
meat mallet, gently pound chicken, one at
a time, between pieces of plastic wrap until
about 5mm thick. Divide herb mixture among
chicken pieces; roll to enclose filling, wrapping
each roll with prosciutto slice to secure.
3 Cook chicken in heated lightly oiled large
frying pan, uncovered, about 10 minutes or
until browned all over. Place chicken on oven
tray; cook, uncovered, in oven, 15 minutes or
until chicken is cooked through.
4 Meanwhile, cook tomatoes in same pan,
over high heat, stirring, 3 minutes. Gently toss
tomatoes, spinach and coarsely chopped basil
in large bowl with combined vinegar and oil.
Serve salad with chicken.

PROSCIUTTO-WRAPPED LAMB WITH ROASTED KIPFLERS

prep & cook time **45 minutes** serves **4**
nutritional count per serving **7.3g total fat**
(3.3g saturated fat); 1488kJ (356 cal);
33.7g carbohydrate; 34.8g protein; 7.3g fibre

800g kipfler potatoes, halved lengthways
400g lamb backstraps
2 cloves garlic, sliced finely
4 slices prosciutto (60g)
300g green beans, trimmed
2 ruby red grapefruits (700g), segmented
½ cup coarsely chopped fresh
    flat-leaf parsley
60g reduced-fat fetta cheese, crumbled

1 Preheat oven to 220°C/200°C fan-forced.
2 Place potato in small ovenproof dish; roast, uncovered, 15 minutes.
3 Meanwhile, cut small slits in lamb; fill each slit with a garlic slice. Wrap prosciutto around lamb. Cook lamb in heated medium frying pan, 1 minute each side. Remove lamb from pan, place on top of potato; return dish to oven, roast lamb and potato, uncovered, about 10 minutes.
4 Meanwhile, boil, steam or microwave beans until tender. Combine beans with remaining ingredients in medium bowl.
5 Slice lamb; serve with potato and salad.

TROPICAL FRUIT
WITH ORANGE GLAZE

prep & cook time 20 minutes serves 4
nutritional count per serving 0.3g total fat
(0g saturated fat); 640kJ (153 cal);
32.1g carbohydrate; 2.8g protein; 4.8g fibre

1 teaspoon finely grated orange rind
2 tablespoons orange juice
2 tablespoons brown sugar
1 small pineapple (900g), trimmed, halved,
   sliced thickly
2 medium bananas (400g), quartered
1 starfruit (160g), sliced thickly
¼ cup loosely packed fresh mint leaves

1 To make orange glaze, combine rind, juice
and sugar in small saucepan; stir over low heat
until sugar dissolves. Cool.
2 Preheat grill.
3 Combine glaze with fruit in large bowl. Spread
fruit mixture onto two foil-lined oven trays.
4 Grill fruit about 5 minutes or until browned
lightly. Serve fruit sprinkled with mint.

BERRY-MUESLI BAKED APPLES

prep & cook time **1 hour 10 minutes** serves **4**
nutritional count per serving **5.4g total fat
(2.9g saturated fat); 681kJ (163 cal);
26g carbohydrate; 1.4g protein; 4.4g fibre**

**4 large granny smith apples (800g)
cooking-oil spray
⅓ cup (35g) natural muesli
½ cup (75g) fresh blueberries
20g butter, melted
3 teaspoons brown sugar**

1 Preheat oven to 160°C/140°C fan-forced.
2 Core unpeeled apples about three-quarters
of the way down from stem end, making hole
4cm in diameter. Use small sharp knife to score
around centre of each apple; lightly spray each
apple with oil.
3 Combine remaining ingredients in small
bowl. Divide mixture among apples, pressing
firmly into holes; place apples in small baking
dish. Bake, uncovered, about 45 minutes or
until apples are just softened.

tea-spiced pears

TEA-SPICED PEARS

prep & cook time **35 minutes** serves **4**
nutritional count per serving **0.1g total fat
(0g saturated fat); 673kJ (161 cal);
37.5g carbohydrate; 6.4g protein; 2.6g fibre**

**1 tablespoon jasmine tea leaves
⅓ cup (75g) firmly packed brown sugar
1 litre (4 cups) boiling water
4 small pears (720g)
2 cinnamon sticks
2 star anise**

1 Combine tea leaves, sugar and the water in
large heatproof jug; stir until sugar dissolves.
Stand 10 minutes. Strain; discard leaves.
2 Meanwhile, peel, halve and core pears.
Combine pears, strained tea mixture and
spices in medium saucepan; bring to the boil.
Simmer, uncovered, about 25 minutes or until
pears are tender. Place pears in serving bowls.
Boil syrup, uncovered, until reduced by half.
3 Serve pears with syrup.
note **You need about four jasmine tea bags to get
one tablespoon of tea leaves.**

PASSIONFRUIT LIME FROZEN YOGURT

prep & cook time 15 minutes
(+ freezing and standing) serves 4
nutritional count per serving 0.4g total fat
(0.1g saturated fat); 853kJ (204 cal);
37.5g carbohydrate; 9.9g protein; 4.4g fibre

½ cup (110g) caster sugar
¼ cup (60ml) water
1 teaspoon powdered gelatine
2 cups (560g) low-fat natural yogurt
½ cup (125ml) passionfruit pulp
1 teaspoon finely grated lime rind
1 tablespoon lime juice

1 Stir sugar and the water in small saucepan over medium heat until sugar dissolves; transfer to large heatproof jug.

2 Sprinkle gelatine over sugar syrup; stir until gelatine dissolves.

3 Stir yogurt, pulp, rind and juice into syrup. Pour yogurt mixture into loaf pan, cover with foil; freeze 3 hours or until almost set. Scrape yogurt from bottom and sides of pan with fork; return to freezer until firm.

4 Stand at room temperature 20 minutes before serving.

WATERMELON, BERRY AND MINT FRAPPÉ

prep time **5 minutes** serves **2**
nutritional count per serving **0.3g total fat**
(0g saturated fat); 167kJ (40 cal);
7.1g carbohydrate; 1.5g protein; 1.4g fibre

Blend or process 400g coarsely chopped seedless watermelon, 125g strawberries and 1 tablespoon lime juice until smooth; transfer to medium jug. Crush 20 ice cubes; stir ice into watermelon mixture. Garnish with fresh mint leaves, if you like.

PEACH AND RASPBERRY JUICE

prep time **5 minutes** serves **1**
nutritional count per serving **0.3g total fat**
(0.6g saturated fat); 314kJ (75 cal);
13.7g carbohydrate; 1.9g protein; 4.1g fibre

Blend or process 1 coarsely chopped large peach and ¼ cup fresh or frozen raspberries until smooth; pour into glass. Stir in ½ cup water; serve with ice.

PASSIONFRUIT SPARKLER

prep time **10 minutes (+ freezing)** serves **4**
nutritional count per serving **0.5g total fat**
(0g saturated fat); 723kJ (173 cal);
31.1g carbohydrate; 4.1g protein; 13.2g fibre

Pour 2 x 170g cans passionfruit in syrup into ice-cube trays; freeze. Segment 1 medium orange and halve 150g seedless red grapes. Combine fruit with passionfruit cubes, 1½ cups pineapple juice, 1½ cups orange juice and 1 cup sparkling mineral water in large jug.

APPLE, PEAR AND GINGER JUICE

prep time **5 minutes** serves **1**
nutritional count per serving **0.3g total fat**
(0g saturated fat); 723kJ (173 cal);
31.1g carbohydrate; 4.1g protein; 13.2g fibre

Push 1 cored and coarsely chopped medium apple, 1 cored and coarsely chopped medium pear and 1cm piece fresh ginger through juice extractor into glass; serve with ice.

JUICES

PINEAPPLE, CARROT AND BEETROOT JUICE

prep time **5 minutes** serves **1**
nutritional count per serving **0.3g total fat**
(0g saturated fat); 439kJ (105 cal);
20.7g carbohydrate; 2.8g protein; 3.5g fibre

Push ¼ peeled and chopped small pineapple,
2 coarsely chopped medium carrots and
1 coarsely chopped small beetroot through
juice extractor into glass. Stir in 2 tablespoons
water and 1 tablespoon lime juice.

WATERCRESS, BEETROOT AND CELERY JUICE

prep time **5 minutes** serves **1**
nutritional count per serving **0.4g total fat**
(0g saturated fat); 222kJ (53 cal);
8.9g carbohydrate; 3.5g protein; 6g fibre

Push 1 coarsely chopped trimmed celery
stalk, 3 coarsely chopped baby beetroots
and 50g trimmed watercress through juice
extractor into glass; stir in ½ cup water.

CARROT, ORANGE AND GINGER JUICE

prep time **5 minutes** serves **1**
nutritional count per serving **0.3g total fat**
(0g saturated fat); 506kJ (121 cal);
22.6g carbohydrate; 3g protein; 0.2g fibre

Push 1 peeled and quartered large orange,
1 coarsely chopped medium carrot and 1cm
piece fresh ginger through juice extractor into
glass. Serve with ice.

PINEAPPLE, ORANGE AND STRAWBERRY JUICE

prep time **5 minutes** serves **1**
nutritional count per serving **0.3g total fat**
(0g saturated fat); 468kJ (112cal);
23.2g carbohydrate; 3.5g protein; 6.6g fibre

Push 1 peeled and quartered small orange,
150g coarsely chopped pineapple and
2 hulled strawberries through juice extractor
into glass; stir in ¼ cup water.

STRAWBERRY PAVLOVAS

prep & cook time **45 minutes (+ cooling)** serves **4**
nutritional count per serving **0.2g total fat
(0g saturated fat); 803kJ (192 cal);
40.4g carbohydrate; 5.3g protein; 2.5g fibre**

**2 egg whites
½ cup (110g) caster sugar
250g strawberries
1 teaspoon wheaten cornflour
1 small banana (130g), chopped finely
1 kiwifruit (85g), chopped finely
½ cup (140g) low-fat passionfruit yogurt**

1 Preheat oven to 140°C/120°C fan-forced.
Line oven tray with baking paper.
2 Beat egg whites in small bowl with electric
mixer until soft peaks form. Gradually add sugar,
one tablespoon at a time, beating until sugar
dissolves between additions.
3 Meanwhile, push four strawberries through a
fine sieve into small bowl (you need 1 tablespoon
of strawberry puree); discard solids.
4 Fold cornflour then strawberry puree into
egg-white mixture. Spoon mixture onto tray;
form mixture into four nests.
5 Bake 10 minutes. Reduce oven temperature
to 120°C/100°C fan-forced. Bake a further
20 minutes. Turn off oven; cool pavlovas in
oven with door ajar.
6 Finely chop remaining strawberries. Combine
strawberries, banana and kiwifruit in medium
bowl. Serve pavlovas topped with yogurt and
fruit mixture.

rhubarb soufflé

RHUBARB SOUFFLÉ

prep & cook time **30 minutes** serves **4**
nutritional count per serving **1.1g total fat**
(0.1g saturated fat); 635kJ (152 cal);
31g carbohydrate; 3.3g protein; 1.3g fibre

cooking-oil spray
½ cup (110g) caster sugar
1½ cups (165g) coarsely chopped rhubarb
1 tablespoon water
3 egg whites
1 tablespoon icing sugar

1 Preheat oven to 200°C/180°C fan-forced.
2 Lightly spray inside of four 1-cup (250ml)
ovenproof dishes with oil. Sprinkle base and
sides of dishes with 2 tablespoons of the
caster sugar. Stand dishes on oven tray.
3 Combine rhubarb, 2 tablespoons of the
caster sugar and the water in small saucepan.
Cook, stirring, over medium heat, about
10 minutes or until mixture thickens. Transfer
mixture to medium heatproof bowl.
4 Meanwhile, beat egg whites in small bowl
with electric mixer until soft peaks form.
Gradually add remaining caster sugar; beat
until firm peaks form.
5 Fold egg-white mixture into warm rhubarb
mixture, in two batches. Spoon mixture into
dishes. Bake, in oven, about 12 minutes.
6 Serve soufflés immediately, dusted with
sifted icing sugar.
note **Rhubarb has thick, celery-like stalks that**
can reach 60cm long; the stalks are the only
edible portion of the plant – the leaves contain
a toxic substance and should be discarded.

caramelised figs with spiced yogurt

CARAMELISED FIGS WITH SPICED YOGURT

prep & cook time **20 minutes** serves **4**
nutritional count per serving **6g total fat**
(1.3g saturated fat); 777kJ (186 cal);
26.1g carbohydrate; 6.8g protein; 3.6g fibre

1 cup (280g) low-fat yogurt
¼ cup (35g) roasted pistachios,
   chopped coarsely
¼ teaspoon ground nutmeg
1 tablespoon caster sugar
6 large fresh figs (480g)
1 tablespoon honey

1 Combine yogurt, nuts, nutmeg and sugar in
small bowl.
2 Halve figs lengthways. Brush cut-side of figs
with honey.
3 Cook figs, cut-side down, uncovered, in
heated large frying pan 5 minutes. Turn figs;
cook, uncovered, 5 minutes or until browned
lightly. Serve figs with spiced yogurt.

ARBORIO RICE small, round-grained rice, able to absorb a large amount of liquid.

ALLSPICE also known as pimento or jamaican pepper; available whole or ground. Tastes like a blend of cinnamon, clove and nutmeg.

ALMOND MEAL also known as ground almonds; nuts are powdered to a coarse flour-like texture.

BACON, SHORTCUT is a "half rasher"; the streaky (belly), narrow portion of the rasher has been removed leaving the choice cut eye meat (fat end).

BASIL an aromatic herb; there are many types, but the most commonly used is sweet, or common, basil.

BEANS

> **broad** also known as fava, windsor and horse beans. Fresh and frozen forms should be peeled twice, discarding both the outer long green pod and the beige-green tough inner shell.

> **four bean mix** a mix of kidney beans, butter beans, chickpeas and cannellini beans.

> **white** in this book, some recipes may simply call for "white beans", a generic term we use for canned or dried cannellini, haricot, navy or great northern beans, all of which can be substituted for each other.

> **yellow** look like green beans without the chlorophyll. As a result they taste less "green" and are slightly less flavoursome than green-coloured beans.

BEEF SKIRT STEAK lean, flavourful coarse-grained cut from the inner thigh. Needs slow-cooking; good for stews or casseroles.

BEETROOT red beets or beets; firm, round root vegetable.

BREAD

> **lavash** (lavosh) a flat, unleavened bread of Mediterranean origin.

> **mountain** thin, dry, soft-textured flat bread used for sandwiches or filled and rolled as a wrap. Available from supermarkets and health-food stores.

> **tortillas** thin, round unleavened bread originating in Mexico. Two types are available, one made from wheat flour and the other from corn.

BUCKWHEAT a herb in the same plant family as rhubarb; not a cereal so it is gluten-free. Available as flour; ground (cracked) into coarse, medium or fine grain; or as groats, the roasted whole kernels cooked similarly to rice or couscous.

BURGHUL also known as bulghur or bulgar wheat; hulled steamed wheat kernels that, once dried, are crushed into various-sized grains. Not the same as cracked wheat. Found in most supermarkets and health-food stores.

BUTTER use salted or unsalted (sweet) butter; 125g is equal to one stick (4 ounces) of butter.

BUTTERMILK originally the term given to the slightly sour liquid left after butter was churned from cream, today it is made similarly to yogurt. Sold alongside fresh milk products in supermarkets. Despite its name, it is low in fat.

BUTTERNUT PUMPKIN (squash) pear-shaped with golden skin and orange flesh.

CAPERS the grey-green buds of a warm climate shrub (usually Mediterranean); sold either dried and salted or pickled in a vinegar brine. Baby capers are very small, and fuller-flavoured than the full-size ones. Rinsed well before using.

CAPSICUM also known as bell pepper or, simply, pepper. Comes in several colours; seeds and membranes should be discarded before use.

CAYENNE PEPPER a long, thin-fleshed, extremely hot red chilli usually sold dried and ground.

CHICKPEAS also called garbanzos, channa or hummus; round, sandy-coloured legume.

CHILLI available in many different types and sizes. Use rubber gloves when seeding and chopping fresh chillies as they can burn your skin. Removing seeds and membranes lessens the heat level.

> **flakes, dried** deep-red, dehydrated chilli slices and whole seeds.

> **long red** available fresh and dried; a generic term used for any long (6cm-8cm), moderately hot, thin chilli.

> **red thai** small, medium hot and bright red in colour.

CORIANDER also known as pak chee, cilantro or chinese parsley; bright-green leafy herb with a pungent flavour. Both the stems and roots of coriander are also used in cooking; wash well before using. Also available ground or as seeds; these should not be substituted for fresh coriander as the tastes are completely different.

CORNFLOUR also known as cornstarch. Available as 100% maize (corn) and wheaten cornflour.

CRANBERRIES, DRIED have the same slightly sour, succulent flavour as fresh cranberries. They are available from supermarkets.

CUMIN a spice also known as zeera or comino; has a spicy, nutty flavour.

EGGPLANT purple-skinned vegetable also known as aubergine.

FENNEL BULB also known as anise or finocchio; a white to very pale green-white, firm, crisp, roundish vegetable about 8-12cm in diameter. Has a slightly sweet, anise flavour but the leaves have a much stronger taste. Also the name given to dried seeds having a licorice flavour.

GLOSSARY

FIRM WHITE FISH FILLETS blue eye, bream, flathead, swordfish, ling, whiting, jewfish, snapper or sea perch are all good choices. Check for small pieces of bone in the fillets and use tweezers to remove them.

FLOUR

plain an all-purpose wheat flour.

self-raising plain or wholemeal flour combined with baking powder in the proportion of 1 cup flour to 2 teaspoons baking powder.

wholemeal milled from whole wheat grain (includes the outer bran layer). Available as plain or self-raising.

FRÛCHE the brand name of a light, fresh French cheese (fromage frais); it has the consistency of thick yogurt with a refreshing, slightly tart taste and a smooth, creamy texture.

GELATINE we use powdered gelatine. It is also available in sheet form, known as leaf gelatine.

GINGER also known as green or root ginger; the root of a tropical plant.

ground also known as powdered ginger; used as a flavouring in cakes and puddings but cannot be substituted for fresh ginger.

KIWIFRUIT also known as chinese gooseberry. Has a brown, somewhat hairy skin and bright-green or yellow flesh with a unique sweet-tart flavour.

LEBANESE CUCUMBER short, slender and thin-skinned. Probably the most popular variety because of its tender, edible skin, tiny, yielding seeds, and sweet, fresh taste.

LEMON GRASS a tall, clumping, lemon-smelling and -tasting, sharp-edged grass; the white lower part of each stem is chopped and used in cooking.

LINGUINE a long, narrow pasta often thought of as a "flat" spaghetti.

MARINARA MIX uncooked, chopped seafood available from fish markets and larger supermarkets.

MESCLUN a mixture of assorted young lettuce and other green leaves.

MILK

rice usually made from filtered water and brown rice. It has less protein and calcium than cow's milk, but is high in carbohydrates and contains no cholesterol or lactose. Rice milk is not as thick as dairy or soy milks, and has a somewhat translucent consistency and a slightly sweet flavour.

skim has less than or equal to 0.1 per cent fat. Sometimes milk solids may be added to optimise the taste. Is sometimes labelled as "no-fat".

soy a rich creamy "milk" extracted from soya beans that have been crushed in hot water and strained. It has a nutty flavour.

MINCE also known as ground meat.

MIRIN sweet rice wine used in Japanese cooking; not to be confused with sake.

MUESLI also known as granola, a combination of grains (mainly oats), nuts and dried fruits. Some varieties may be toasted in oil and honey, adding crispness and kilojoules.

MUSHROOMS, FLAT large, flat mushrooms with a rich earthy flavour. They are sometimes misnamed field mushrooms, which are wild mushrooms.

MUSTARD

dijon a pale brown, distinctively flavoured, fairly mild tasting french mustard.

wholegrain also known as seeded mustard. A French-style coarse-grain mustard made from crushed mustard seeds and dijon-style french mustard.

NOODLES, BEAN THREAD made from dried mung bean flour. Are very fine, almost transparent noodles also known as bean thread vermicelli, or cellophane or glass noodles.

OCEAN TROUT a farmed fish with pink, soft flesh. It is from the same family as the atlantic salmon; one can be substituted for the other.

OIL

cooking spray we use a cholesterol-free canola oil.

olive made from ripened olives. Extra virgin and virgin are the best, while extra light or light refers to taste not fat levels.

peanut pressed from peanuts; has a high smoke point (able to handle high heat without burning).

walnut pressed from walnuts. Available from delicatessens, some major supermarkets and gourmet food stores.

ONIONS

green also known as scallion or, incorrectly, shallot; an immature onion picked before the bulb has formed, having a long, bright-green edible stalk.

red also known as spanish, red spanish or bermuda onion; a sweet-flavoured, large, purple-red onion.

PAPRIKA a ground, dried, sweet red capsicum (bell pepper); there are many types available, including sweet, hot, mild and smoked.

PARSLEY, FLAT-LEAF also known as continental or italian parsley.

PEARL BARLEY barley that has had the husk removed, then been hulled and polished, similarly to rice.

PISTACHIOS pale green, delicately flavoured nut inside hard off-white shells. To peel, soak shelled nuts in boiling water for about 5 minutes; drain, then pat dry with absorbent paper. Rub skins with cloth to peel.

POTATOES

baby new also known as chats; not a separate variety but an early harvest with very thin skin.

kipfler small, finger-shaped potato having a nutty flavour.

PRAWNS also known as shrimp.

PROSCIUTTO cured, air-dried (unsmoked), pressed ham.

RICE PAPER SHEETS also known as banh trang. Made from rice paste and stamped into rounds. Dipped momentarily in water they become pliable wrappers for fried food and uncooked vegetables. Make good spring-roll wrappers.

ROCKET also known as arugula, rugula and rucola; a peppery-tasting green leaf that can be eaten raw in salads or used in cooking. Baby rocket, also known as wild rocket, is both smaller and less peppery.

ROLLED OATS oat groats (oats that have been husked) steamed-softened, flattened with rollers then dried and packaged.

RUBY RED GRAPEFRUIT has pink flesh and is slightly sweeter than the common yellow variety.

SAUCES

fish also called nam pla or nuoc nam; made from pulverised salted fermented fish, most often anchovies. Has a pungent smell and strong taste, so use sparingly.

hoisin a thick, sweet and spicy Chinese sauce made from onions, garlic and fermented soya beans.

soy made from fermented soya beans. Several variations are available in most supermarkets and Asian food stores.

japanese soy we use japanese soy, unless indicated otherwise: an all-purpose low-sodium soy sauce fermented in barrels and aged. Made with more wheat content than its Chinese counterparts and is possibly the best table soy to choose if you only want one variety.

kecap manis a dark, thick sweet soy sauce. The sweetness is from the addition of either molasses or palm sugar when brewed.

light soy a fairly thin, pale but salty tasting sauce; used in dishes in which the natural colour of the ingredients is to be maintained. Not to be confused with salt-reduced or low-sodium soy sauces.

sweet chilli a comparatively mild, Thai sauce made from red chillies, sugar, garlic and vinegar.

teriyaki a Japanese sauce made from soy sauce, mirin, sugar, ginger and other spices. Used as a glaze to brush over meat or poultry.

tomato pasta a prepared sauce made from a blend of tomatoes, herbs and spices.

SNOW PEAS also called mange tout ("eat all").

snow pea sprouts tender new growths of snow peas.

SPINACH also known as english spinach and, incorrectly, silver beet.

SPLIT PEAS a variety of yellow or green pea grown specifically for drying. When dried, the peas usually split along a natural seam. Whole and split dried peas are available packaged in supermarkets and in bulk from health-food stores.

STAR ANISE dried, star-shaped pod having an astringent aniseed flavour. Available whole and ground; is an ingredient in five-spice powder.

STARFRUIT also known as chinese starfruit, carambola or five-corner fruit; a pale-green or yellow colour. Has a clean, crisp texture, but the flavour may be either sweet or sour, depending on the variety and when picked. No need to peel or seed. Are slow to discolour; avoid ones with brown spots or streaks.

SUGAR

brown a soft, finely granulated sugar retaining molasses for its characteristic colour and flavour.

caster also known as superfine or finely granulated table sugar.

icing also known as confectioners' sugar or powdered sugar; granulated sugar crushed together with a small amount of added cornflour.

white a coarse, granulated table sugar, also known as crystal sugar.

TOFU also known as bean curd, an off-white, custard-like product made from the "milk" of crushed soya beans; comes fresh as soft or firm. Refrigerate leftover fresh tofu in water (which is changed daily) for up to 4 days. Silken refers to the method by which it is made – where it is strained through silk.

VANILLA EXTRACT made by pulping vanilla beans with a mixture of alcohol and water. This gives a very strong solution, and only a couple of drops are needed.

VINEGAR

balsamic made from the juice of Trebbiano grapes; has a rich brown colour and a sweet and sour flavour.

balsamic, white (condiment) is a clear, lighter version of balsamic vinegar; has a fresh, sweet taste.

cider (apple cider) made from fermented apples.

raspberry fresh raspberries are steeped in a white wine vinegar.

red wine based on fermented red wine.

white wine made from a blend of white wines.

WOMBOK also known as peking, chinese or petsai cabbage. Elongated in shape with pale green, crinkly leaves; the most common cabbage in South-East Asia.

WONTON WRAPPERS also known as wonton skins. Found in the refrigerated section of supermarkets and Asian grocery stores; gow gee, egg or spring roll pastry sheets can be substituted.

ZUCCHINI also known as courgette; belongs to the squash family.

CONVERSION CHART

MEASURES

One Australian metric measuring cup holds approximately 250ml, one Australian metric tablespoon holds 20ml, one Australian metric teaspoon holds 5ml.

The difference between one country's measuring cups and another's is within a 2- or 3-teaspoon variance, and will not affect your cooking results. North America, New Zealand and the United Kingdom use a 15ml tablespoon. All cup and spoon measurements are level. The most accurate way of measuring dry ingredients is to weigh them. When measuring liquids, use a clear glass or plastic jug with metric markings.

We use large eggs with an average weight of 60g.

DRY MEASURES

METRIC	IMPERIAL
15g	½oz
30g	1oz
60g	2oz
90g	3oz
125g	4oz (¼lb)
155g	5oz
185g	6oz
220g	7oz
250g	8oz (½lb)
280g	9oz
315g	10oz
345g	11oz
375g	12oz (¾lb)
410g	13oz
440g	14oz
470g	15oz
500g	16oz (1lb)
750g	24oz (1½lb)
1kg	32oz (2lb)

LIQUID MEASURES

METRIC	IMPERIAL
30ml	1 fluid oz
60ml	2 fluid oz
100ml	3 fluid oz
125ml	4 fluid oz
150ml	5 fluid oz (¼ pint/1 gill)
190ml	6 fluid oz
250ml	8 fluid oz
300ml	10 fluid oz (½ pint)
500ml	16 fluid oz
600ml	20 fluid oz (1 pint)
1000ml (1 litre)	1¾ pints

LENGTH MEASURES

METRIC	IMPERIAL
3mm	⅛in
6mm	¼in
1cm	½in
2cm	¾in
2.5cm	1in
5cm	2in
6cm	2½in
8cm	3in
10cm	4in
13cm	5in
15cm	6in
18cm	7in
20cm	8in
23cm	9in
25cm	10in
28cm	11in
30cm	12in (1ft)

OVEN TEMPERATURES

These oven temperatures are only a guide for conventional ovens.
For fan-forced ovens, check the manufacturer's manual.

	°C (CELSIUS)	°F (FAHRENHEIT)	GAS MARK
Very slow	120	250	½
Slow	150	275-300	1-2
Moderately slow	160	325	3
Moderate	180	350-375	4-5
Moderately hot	200	400	6
Hot	220	425-450	7-8
Very hot	240	475	9

INDEX

ACP BOOKS
General manager Christine Whiston
Editor-in-chief Susan Tomnay
Creative director Hieu Chi Nguyen
Art director & designer Hannah Blackmore
Senior editor Wendy Bryant
Food director Pamela Clark
Food editor + nutritional information Rebecca Squadrito
Sales & rights director Brian Cearnes
Marketing manager Bridget Cody
Senior business analyst Rebecca Varela
Circulation manager Jarna Mclean
Operations manager David Scotto
Production manager Victoria Jefferys

ACP Books are published by ACP Magazines
a division of PBL Media Pty Limited
PBL Media, Chief Executive officer Ian Law
Publishing & sales director, Women's lifestyle Lynette Phillips
General manager, Editorial projects, Women's lifestyle Deborah Thomas
Group editorial director, Women's lifestyle Pat Ingram
Marketing director, Women's lifestyle Matthew Dominello
Commercial manager, Women's lifestyle Seymour Cohen
Research Director, Women's lifestyle Justin Stone

Produced by ACP Books, Sydney.

Published by ACP Books, a division of ACP Magazines Ltd, 54 Park St, Sydney; GPO Box 4088, Sydney, NSW 2001.
phone (02) 9282 8618; fax (02) 9267 9438. acpbooks@acpmagazines.com.au; www.acpbooks.com.au

Printed by Toppan Printing Co., China.

Australia Distributed by Network Services, phone +61 2 9282 8777;
fax +61 2 9264 3278; networkweb@networkservicescompany.com.au
United Kingdom Distributed by Australian Consolidated Press (UK), phone (01604) 642 200;
fax (01604) 642 300; books@acpuk.com
New Zealand Distributed by Netlink Distribution Company, phone (9) 366 9966; ask@ndc.co.nz
South Africa Distributed by PSD Promotions, phone (27 11) 392 6065/6/7;
fax (27 11) 392 6079/80; orders@psdprom.co.za
Canada Distributed by Publishers Group Canada
phone (800) 663 5714; fax (800) 565 3770; service@raincoast.com

Low fat kitchen/food director Pamela Clark.
ISBN: 978 1 74245 006 3
A catalogue record for this book is available
from the British Library.
© ACP Magazines Ltd 2010
ABN 18 053 273 546

Cover Corn fritters, page 12
Photographer Ian Wallace
Stylist Louise Pickford
Food preparation Rebecca Squadrito

Send recipe enquiries to: recipeenquiries@acpmagazines.com.au